Buffy the Vampire Slayer™

the

Essential Angel

POCKET BOOKS

New York   London   Toronto   Sydney   Tokyo   Singapore

An *Original* Publication of Pocket Books

 POCKET BOOKS, a division of Simon & Schuster Inc.
1230 Avenue of the Americas, New York, NY 10020

ISBN: 0-671-03653-X

First Pocket Books trade paperback printing April 1999

10 9 8 7 6 5 4 3

POCKET and colophon are registered trademarks
of Simon & Schuster Inc.

Designed by Lili Schwartz

Printed in the U.S.A.

Angel: "I want to learn from you."

Whistler: "Okay."

Angel: "But I don't want to dress like you."

—**"BECOMING, PART 1"**

Jenny: "You were born to hurt her. Have you learned nothing? As long as you're alive—"

Angel: "Then I'll die."

Jenny: "You don't have the strength to kill yourself.

Angel: "I don't need strength. I just need the sun to rise."

—"**AMENDS**"

Buffy: "How did you find me here?"

Angel: "If I was blind, I would see you."

Buffy: "Stay with me."

Angel: "Forever. That's the whole point. I'll never leave. Not even if you kill me."

— "ANNE"

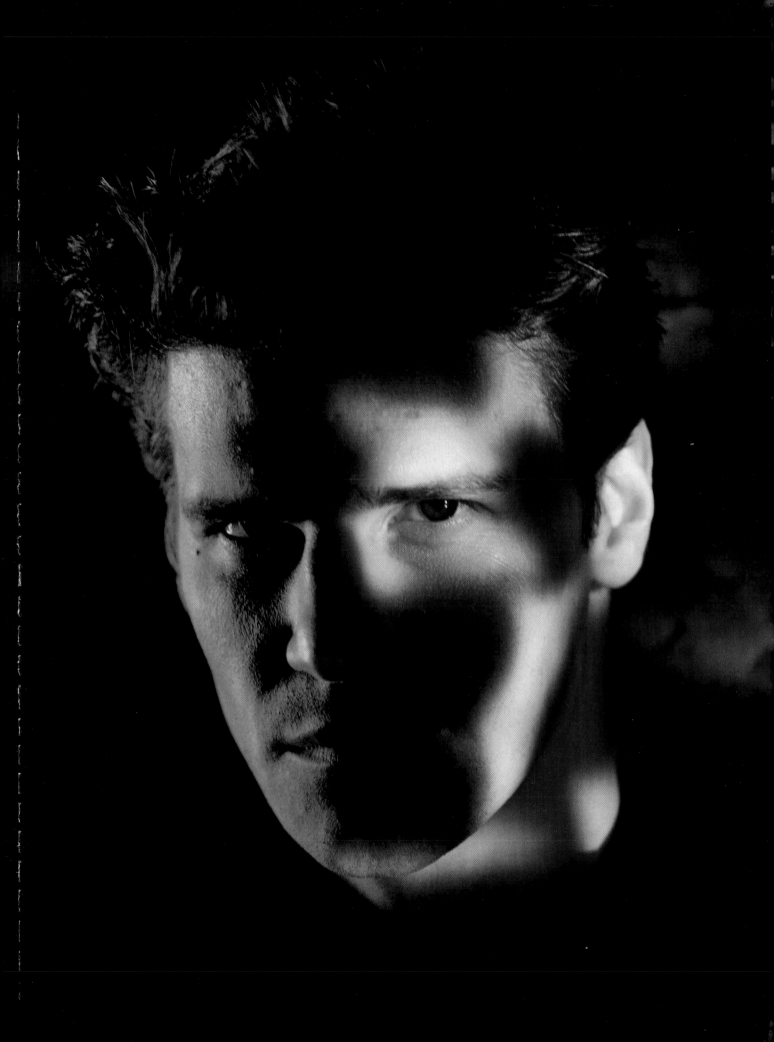

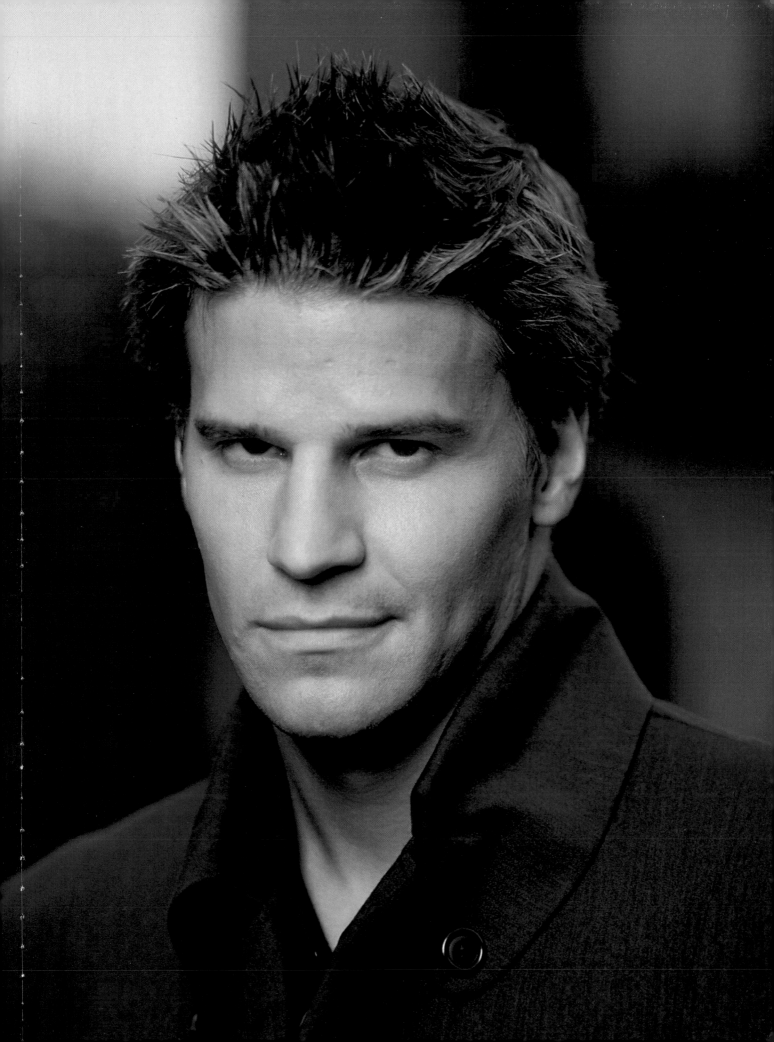

"There is a lot to [Angel] that I would like to explore. He's got a good side and he's got a bad side. How you keep that balanced is pretty interesting. Sure, he can mope around and be sad and brooding. Or he can try to make a difference, somehow, in somebody's life. You know what I'm saying? Sure, you can make your amends and go on with it."

—DAVID BOREANAZ
interview excerpted from *The Watcher's Guide: The Official Companion to the Hit Show*
By Christopher Golden and Nancy Holder

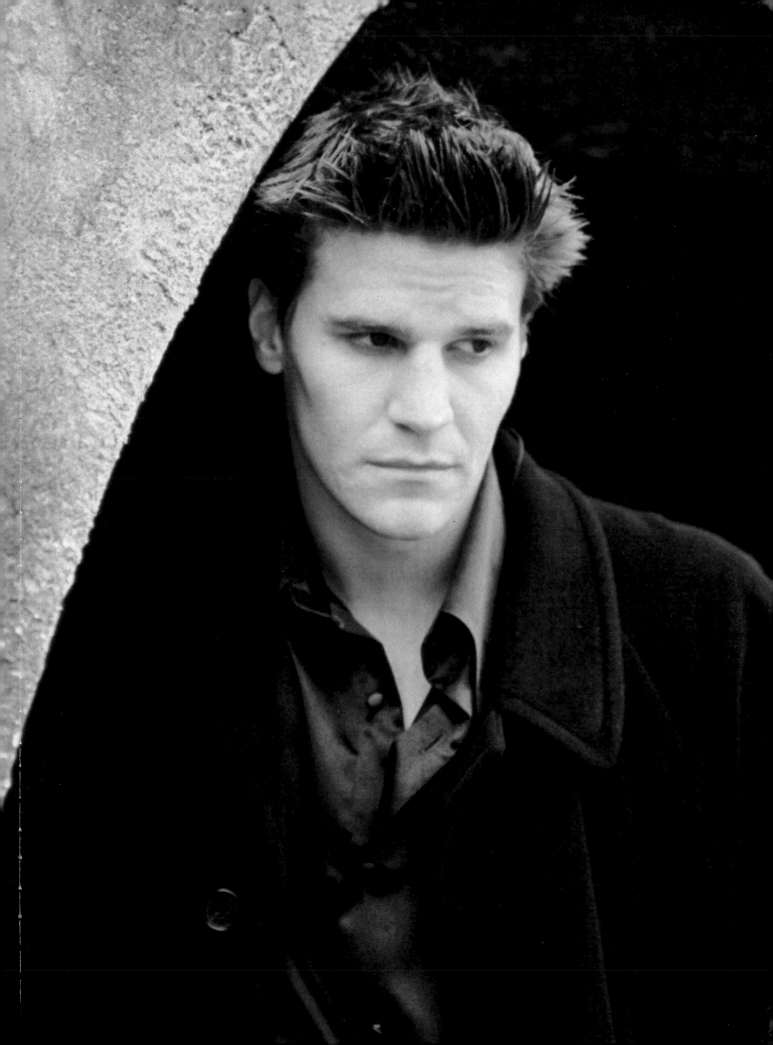

Buffy: "I invited you into my home. And then you attacked my family."

Angel: "Why not? I killed mine. I killed their friends and their friends' children. For a hundred years, I offered an ugly death to everyone I met. And I did it with a song in my heart."

—"ANGEL"